Original title:
Life's Not That Complicated (or Is It?)

Copyright © 2025 Creative Arts Management OÜ
All rights reserved.

Author: Theodore Sinclair
ISBN HARDBACK: 978-1-80566-013-2
ISBN PAPERBACK: 978-1-80566-308-9

The Quiet Uproar Within

Inside my brain, a circus thrives,
Clowns are laughing, juggling lives.
I try to focus, but what's the use?
Pinball thoughts go on the loose.

What's for dinner? Where's my sock?
A riddle wrapped in a paradox.
I sip my drink, and then it spills,
Just like my thoughts, full of thrills.

On the Brink of Understanding

I ponder deep at 2 AM,
Why does my cat think she's a gem?
The toaster burns, but my heart is warm,
   Riding waves of chaotic charm.

In the kitchen, pots perform a dance,
Will I succeed or miss my chance?
With noodles boiling, I hear a tune,
   Maybe it's just the silver spoons.

The Harmony of Confusion

Lost in thoughts like a maze of cheese,
When it's sunny, I wear my freeze.
The dog chases shadows with great flair,
Who knew that life could be such a dare?

I trip on air and search for reason,
It's not the same in every season.
A laugh escapes, I scratch my head,
Found joking truth in things unsaid.

Scribbles of the Heart

With crayons vibrant, I sketch my plight,
How to make sense of the delightful night?
Love's a puzzle, not pieces missing,
In jumbled notes, I find my wishing.

The heart writes songs, in scribbles bold,
Of awkward moments and stories told.
In laughter's echo, I seek my part,
A comic play of the wandering heart.

Beneath the Surface of Complexity

In a world full of twists and bends,
We juggle like clowns, overlook our friends.
A sandwich order takes ages to unfold,
While secrets of joy lay silently untold.

We seek the map but get lost in the fray,
Like trying to catch a cat on a sunny day.
With layers that peel like onions of yore,
We laugh at the mess, still hungry for more.

The Art of Unraveling

A puzzle begins with pieces amiss,
We chase the corners and reminisce.
Threading the needle of thoughts gone astray,
We poke and we prod as laughter holds sway.

The coffee spills while the cat takes a leap,
Then suddenly we're tangled in thoughts that run deep.
Each twist of the yarn, a new comic relief,
In the grand game of baffling belief.

Whispers of Uncertainty

In shadows of doubt, we tiptoe about,
Silent whispers play tricks, a dainty clout.
With questions that bounce like crazy ping pong,
The right answer feels like it won't come along.

We fumble with words, like walking on eggs,
The punchline we search gives nothing but dregs.
Yet we grin at the mess, for joy is the catch,
In this swirling dance, we happily scratch.

The Fine Line Between Easy and Hard

Sometimes it's fun just to muddle along,
Like brewing a stew that smells slightly wrong.
We trip over thoughts, like an overripe peach,
Unraveling joy that seems just out of reach.

The breeze is a riddle, the sun won't cooperate,
While the dog holds the key to a comical fate.
Between chuckles and sighs, we navigate glee,
A circus of moments, just you and me.

When the Clock Strikes Confusion

Time ticks away, oh what a mess,
Lost in the hours, I must confess.
Coffee's grown cold, the day's in a spin,
Why do we rush, when the fun's about to begin?

Meetings and emails, they come in a rush,
But when I get there, I find no one to crush.
Is this the right place, or did I miss the turn?
I'll just grab a donut, for that I won't yearn.

The Melody of Mixed Signals

A wink, a nod, or maybe it's fate?
I wave to my neighbor, but he thinks it's too late.
Do I say hello, or pretend to not know?
The tune of confusion, just putting on a show.

A text that says 'hi' with a smiley too,
But I send a meme, is that what I do?
Flirting or joking? It's anyone's guess,
In the fog of romance, who can feel less?

Disguised Simplicity

A recipe written, so clear and so bright,
Chopped this and that, it should be a delight.
But salt's in the sugar, and oh what a twist,
Cooking's a journey, a culinary tryst.

"Just follow the steps," they say with a grin,
But directions confuse when you're lost in the din.
Is it one cup of flour or a pinch of despair?
The dish turns to chaos, but who needs a prayer?

The Quest for Clarity in the Storm

Navigating chaos, a map in my hand,
But every direction feels like quicksand.
Lightning and thunder, they dance and they play,
Who knew a drizzle could ruin my day?

The GPS murmurs, "Recalculating your route,"
But my brain is a maze, I'm totally out.
Amidst all the fuss, a laugh bursts free,
In this tangled adventure, I find it's just me.

A Compass in the Chaos

In tangled webs we find our way,
Maps drawn on napkins, bright as day.
Lost in laughter, found in a grin,
Who needs a plan when chaos begins?

Dancing through mishaps, a wild spree,
Stumbling like ducks, but so carefree.
Directions are squeaky, pavement a maze,
Yet in the bewildering, we find our phase.

With GPS blaring, we still take a turn,
Lessons in wrong ways, oh how we learn!
Where are we headed? Who really knows?
Just follow the jester where laughter flows.

So grab your compass, toss it aside,
In the midst of confusion, let joy be your guide.
With smiles as our fuel, oh what a ride,
In this messy adventure, let whimsy preside.

Gossamer Threads of Thought

Thoughts like bubbles float in the air,
Popping with giggles, light as a flare.
We chase the wild fancies, just for the fun,
Each elusive notion, we catch on the run.

Tangled ideas like yarn in a ball,
Rolling around, will we trip or stand tall?
Each thread unwinds, and what do we see?
A tapestry woven with sheer jubilee!

Whispers of silly, echoes of cheer,
Dancing like shadows, always so near.
In glimmers of wisdom, absurdity thrives,
With laughter as fuel, oh how it drives!

So gather your thoughts, let them take flight,
In gossamer dreams, find your delight.
The web may be wild, but let's have a ball,
For the best kind of thinking is joyful for all.

Transitory Trails

On trails of whimsy, we jog and we run,
Each bend in the path hides a new kind of fun.
Steps that are crooked, yet spirits are high,
We trip over roots while the squirrels fly by.

From puddles to puddles, we splash like a child,
Nature's our playground, our laughter is wild.
With sticks as our swords and hats made of grass,
Every moment an adventure, each second a blast.

The journey unfolds with a wink and a nudge,
Every misstep celebrated, no need for a grudge.
With each fleeting moment, we frolic and play,
For trails may be transitory, but joy's here to stay!

So grab your companions, let's wander and roam,
Through fields of hilarity, we'll find our true home.
In the laughter of mischief, together we thrive,
With memories blossoming, forever alive.

Sips of Simplicity

A cup of delight, a dash of surprise,
We sip happiness, toasting the skies.
With flavors of silly, a twist of the mind,
In each little chuckle, joy's what we find.

With sprinkles of laughter and dashes of fun,
Brewing bright moments under the sun.
Take a big gulp, let your worries dissolve,
Simplicity's spark, oh how it evolves!

Each sip tells a story, each laugh is a cheer,
Lingering flavors, we hold them so dear.
In mugs filled with warmth, we savor our fate,
A pinch of absurdity, oh isn't it great?

So fill up your cup, let's drink to the day,
With each little sip, let confusion decay.
In the cozy embrace of the ordinary's glow,
We find all the magic that just wants to grow.

The Labyrinth of Laughter

In mazes of giggles, we often roam,
Chasing our thoughts like a wayward gnome.
Each twist and turn, a chuckle awaits,
With puns and jests, we dance on our fates.

We stumble on words, a comical race,
Falling like pillows, we cushion our grace.
Silly mishaps become joyous jams,
As laughter breaks out like spontaneous clams.

In the halls of humor, we find our way,
Navigating quips that brighten the day.
With friends by our side, the journey's a blast,
In the labyrinth of laughter, joy's unsurpassed.

So let's trip on our jokes, take a giddy spin,
With every misstep, we're grinning within.
For the path to mirth is whimsically wild,
In this funny maze, we're all just a child.

Moments on the Edge of Clarity

Peering through fog, the world feels askew,
Truths hover lightly, just out of view.
A wink from the universe, a puzzling tease,
Questions unravel like vines on the breeze.

In flashes of insight, we giggle and sway,
Ideas mix wildly, a colorful fray.
What's clear as daylight becomes murky and dark,
Dancing on edges with no proper spark.

Yet in this confusion, we find a kind joke,
The answers are hidden, like smoke from a poke.
Just cherish the moments when thoughts intertwine,
For clarity teases, like wine served with thyme.

So toast to confusion, make merry the night,
With every misstep, we find new delight.
The edges are messy, yet beautifully bright,
In moments of chaos, we spark our own light.

Contrasts of the Unremarkable

In the dull of the day, a treasure's concealed,
Simple times sparkle, as laughter is revealed.
An umbrella that's broken, held high in the rain,
Transforms into joy, pleasure mixed with pain.

Fridge magnets wobble, their colors a clash,
Holding memories awkward, in a quirky stash.
From burnt toast to blunders, we savor our flaws,
Finding humor in life's most ridiculous laws.

With socks that don't match, we strut down the street,
Celebrating blunders, our hearts skip a beat.
Embrace every moment, however you can,
For the unremarkable forms our funny plan.

So hail to the mundane, the bizarre and the flat,
Uncover the giggles that cling to the fat.
In the land of contrasts, our happiness grows,
In the ordinary chaos, that's where humor flows.

The Theatre of the Mundane

Welcome to curtains drawn over the drab,
Where the stars are toothpaste and slippers, a fab.
Each scene precedes with a sigh and a sigh,
Turns mundane troubles into comedy high.

A toast to the traffic, the coffee gone cold,
We perform our routines, both honest and bold.
From mishaps to mix-ups, a slapstick delight,
In this theatre of daily, we play every night.

The actors are famished, the audience snores,
Yet each awkward moment opens new doors.
With scripts that are scribbled on napkins with care,
We bask in the laughter that fills the air.

So raise up your glasses to mischief we brew,
In this play of the ordinary, we find joy anew.
For in every routine, a punchline does cling,
In the theatre of mundane, join in and sing!

The Spectrum of Simplicity

In a world of colors bright,
We seek shades of wrong and right.
A jellybean can spark a fight,
Yet laughter reigns, a pure delight.

We complicate with added flair,
Like wearing socks that don't match pair.
Yet in the chaos, we declare,
It's quite alright; we're beyond compare.

An apple pie or a veggie stew,
Which one's better? Who has a clue?
We juggle choices, just a few,
And toast to the absurdity we brew.

So raise a cup to simple things,
To belly laughs and awkward flings.
For in the end, the joy it brings,
Outshines the weight of greater swings.

Unpacking the Unsung

We bury treasure in the mundane,
Like socks and keys lost in the rain.
The silence hums a minor strain,
Yet giggles echo, breaking the chain.

The coffee spills on Tuesday's plot,
A classic tale that we forgot.
We ponder deep what means a lot,
Then laugh at all we've tangled, caught.

The grocery list, a daunting climb,
Where corn and cheese both share a rhyme.
Yet with each tick, we find the time,
To chuckle at our silly prime.

In little moments, we distill,
The humor stirs, a gentle thrill.
Embrace the joy, no need for will,
It's in the quirks that hearts refill.

The Contrast of Calm and Storm

The sun shines bright, then clouds roll in,
One moment peace, the next, a din.
A grilled cheese melt, a guilty sin,
Then rain arrives—oh where've you been?

Our plans are grand, but winds may change,
A dance in puddles feels so strange.
We find a laugh in life's exchange,
As toss-up moments rearrange.

The couch potato turns to race,
In chaos, we quicken our pace.
Yet at the end of every chase,
Is humor found in every place.

So ride the waves, bring on the jest,
A twinkle in our wobbling quest.
For mixed-up fun is truly best,
Amidst the calm and stormy fest.

In Search of the Elusive

A sock, a cat, a missing shoe,
Each day unfolds a mystery new.
We hunt and search, as lost dogs do,
Yet laughter fills the things we rue.

In quests for snacks our hearts will race,
The pantry door, a secret place.
We stand in awe at fishy grace,
And every crab dance makes us brace.

The remote hides well, a crafty beast,
While chores stack up like a giant feast.
But in each mishap, quite the tease,
We find the joke, a sweet release.

So here's to searching and to play,
To finding joy in the fray.
For every lost and found array,
Brings glee that won't just fade away.

Cracks in the Crystal Ball

Peering deep into the glass,
I see a future, oh so vast.
But it cracks and then it twirls,
A waltz of mad and merry swirls.

Fortune tellers scoff and shout,
As wrong predictions spin about.
A parrot squawks the truth to me,
"It's all just nonsense, can't you see?"

I take the plunge, I take a chance,
My plans are more like clumsy dance.
Yet through the mess, I find a way,
To laugh at life, come what may.

So here's to all the silly woes,
To all the twists that life bestows.
Let crystals crack and spirits cheer,
For joy and fun, we hold so dear.

The Hidden in the Haphazard

Amid splotches of chaos bright,
I stumble on the pure delight.
An untamed shoe beneath the bed,
Its partner ruled by dust instead.

A sock parade, mismatched and bold,
Reveals stories waiting to be told.
I trip on laughter, catch a glance,
In haphazard strife, I stand and dance.

The clutter sings a merry tune,
Each misplaced thing hums to the moon.
In every mess, a treasure lies,
A wink of joy in the surprise.

So here's to chaos, wild and free,
To playful paths that lead to glee.
In tangled threads, the fun won't end,
As haphazard turns into a friend.

The Balance of a Fragile World

A teeter-totter, high and low,
One side heavy, the other slow.
Balancing acts with wobbly grace,
In this circus, we find our place.

We juggle tasks with silly flair,
And drop the balls, oh, unaware.
Yet laughter lifts us when we fail,
As we stumble on this crazy trail.

The fragile thread of hopes and dreams,
We weave and knot with silly schemes.
One silly slip could cause a quake,
Yet onward we march, with joy at stake.

So here's to balance, frail but true,
In this dance, there's room for you.
In every wobble, find a gold,
As we laugh at what life has told.

Whirls of Time and Space

Time does a jig; space spins around,
A whirlwind of thoughts that astound.
In cosmic chaos, we all glide,
With silly smiles as our guide.

Each tick of the clock, a funny tune,
Tickling dreams beneath the moon.
Past, present, future all entwined,
As we giggle at what we find.

A comet zooms, a starfish floats,
In swirling midst of wild anecdotes.
We leap through portals, make a fuss,
In this madcap dance, we trust.

So let's embrace the wobbly ride,
With humor dancing by our side.
In whirls of time and space, we play,
And laugh the tangled night away.

Navigating Through the Fog

Woke up today, thought I knew
Where the coffee was brewing, who knew?
But my keys are missing, oh what a mess,
Guess I'll find adventure, just like the rest.

Clouds in my head, maybe it's rain,
Lost my umbrella, now isn't that plain?
I wander through life, like it's a dance,
Tripping on gas cans, just take a chance.

Maps are for scholars, I'll take a ride,
Follow the cat, it won't be denied.
With laughter and chaos, I'll make my way,
Finding sweet moments in the disarray.

So here's to the fog, and the funny plight,
Drifting through chaos, feeling so light.
For even in mishaps—who would have thought—
The craziest journeys are the ones that we sought.

The Balance of Knowing

Sometimes I ponder, yet never decide,
Should I wear a hat, or just take a stride?
With seconds that tick, and choices to make,
I'll flip a coin, oh for goodness' sake!

The fridge is full, but dinner's a joke,
Burnt my toast—was it me or the smoke?
I question my choices, so neat and so clear,
Yet stumble on answers, like socks without pairs.

A puzzle of thoughts, scattered and wide,
With laughter as glue, and joy as my guide.
Who needs a plan when life hands you fun?
Just roll with the punches; we all weigh a ton!

So here's to the madness that keeps us afloat,
Finding balance while blowing a goat!
For knowing so much can sometimes confuse,
Let's laugh at the chaos, and pick which to choose.

Harmony Amidst the Noise

The kettle is whistling, the cat's on the prowl,
My brain's serenading, a curious howl.
Sounds clashing together, like dishes in flight,
Yet somehow I'm dancing, what a delight!

The neighbor is mowing, the kids are so loud,
But I'll grab my towel, and jump in the crowd.
With giggles and rhythms, I'll play my own tune,
Creating small symphonies beneath the bright moon.

In chaos my heart finds a silly refrain,
Solving the riddles, it's never a pain.
Life's quirky notes turn the noise into glee,
A cacophony of laughter, just let it be free.

So here's to the sounds, the wacky parade,
Finding sweet harmony in every charade.
For in all the ruckus, the fun we can glean,
Is the sweetest of music, if you know what I mean.

Searching for the Unseen Path

With vague directions scrawled on my hand,
I stumble around, feeling less than grand.
A map is just paper, what do I care?
I'll follow my nose, see where it leads me there.

Is this left or right? Oh who can tell?
Stumbling through shrubs, I'm under a spell.
Clocks are just suggestions, I'm taking my time,
Exploring the world, a nonsensical rhyme.

The ground feels unsteady, but laughter is near,
When searching for something, I'll lift up my cheer.
For every misstep brings a smile to my face,
As I bumble through life at a comical pace.

So here's to the journeys with twists and with bends,
Finding strange treasures, and quirky new friends.
For when paths are unseen, the fun's just begun,
Let's dive into chaos, it's all part of the fun!

Ripple Effects in Still Waters

A pebble dropped with such a thud,
Creates a splash, a tiny flood.
The fish look up, then swim away,
As chaos reigns, they start to play.

The ripples dance, the ducks just quack,
While frogs debate the meaning back.
A simple drop, yet who would guess,
The pond would turn to such a mess?

In quiet moments, thoughts collide,
A whisper here, a playful tide.
Yet out of madness comes a cheer,
For laughter's close, it's always near.

So toss a stone or two, my friend,
And watch the quirks of fate descend.
In stillness lies the funny truth,
Just sail along, embrace the goof!

Unraveled Thoughts at Dusk

As daylight fades, my mind does roam,
In tangled webs, I find my home.
Should I go left or is it right?
Decisions loom in fading light.

The cat just stares and licks a paw,
While I recount each baffling flaw.
What's for dinner? Pizza or pie?
A simple query, oh my, oh my!

The stars appear like tiny jokes,
Twinkling down on clueless folks.
In the dark, the answers hide,
Yet still I laugh, I won't abide.

So here I sit, with thoughts adrift,
Embracing chaos, what a gift!
In the evening's blend of silly strife,
I wink and smile, this is called life.

Unspoken Rules of the Heart

Oh, love's a game with no clear guide,
With secret codes we try to slide.
A wink, a nod, or just a glance,
Can lead to joy or awkward dance.

We wear our hearts like mismatched socks,
With hidden beats and ticking clocks.
The messages often get lost,
But silly sparks are worth the cost.

With every text, we start to sweat,
Do we reply? Or just forget?
It's equal parts thrill and dread,
As unspoken words sit on the bed.

So here's to all the hearts that thrive,
In spaces where the laughs arrive.
For love is sweet and oft unclear,
But funny moments keep it near.

A Labyrinth of Choices

In a maze of paths, I scratch my head,
With options wide, yet feeling dread.
Should I wear blue or maybe red?
Oh, choices swirl, I'm almost fed!

Each turn I take, there's something new,
Like chocolate cake or spicy stew.
Should I take the plunge or just a peek?
In the web of choice, I feel so meek.

The map is drawn, yet I am lost,
Is this the path, or is it cost?
It's filled with signs that jest and tease,
While I just chuckle, if you please.

So if you find a fork ahead,
Dive into laughter, leave out dread.
In this maze where whims can thrive,
Embrace the twists, that's how we drive!

Hidden Patterns in the Mundane

In coffee cups we find lost dreams,
Cereal spills, and silly schemes.
A sock's a rogue, a shoe's a clown,
As chaos wears a sparkling crown.

The dust bunnies dance in the light,
Mischief-makers in the night.
They gather tales from under chairs,
A secret club with no repairs.

The clock ticks loud, a jokester's chime,
It bends our plans, it steals our time.
Yet in its rhythm, comical beats,
We find the spark in daily feats.

So let's embrace this charming mess,
With laughter bright, we'll find success.
For in the quirks and silly ways,
Each normal night, a laugh displays.

Masquerade of Easy Answers

Wearing masks of wisdom, we act so wise,
Like playful jesters in a grand disguise.
We nod and smile, play along the game,
While questions swirl, but never name.

The guidebook says to simply 'be',
But what's that mean? Oh, can't you see?
We trip on answers, oh so quaint,
Like trying to paint without a paint.

We seek the truth in cookie crumbs,
While slip-ups bring a hundred puns.
Yet in confusion, humor lays,
Like laughter finding its own ways.

So let's misstep and take the fall,
With chuckles loud, we'll have a ball.
For in the search for sense and rhyme,
We'll craft our joy, one silly time.

Echoes of Ordinary Wonders

The fridge hums tunes of a pop song's past,
While crumbs of life stick like questions cast.
An empty jar with stories to tell,
Echoes of laughter from where we fell.

Each day a stage, the antics unfold,
The shopping list gets lost in bold.
Peppers dance with oranges bright,
In this grocery play, what feels so right?

A dog's goofy bark sings the dawn,
As mismatched slippers have a yawn.
In every giggle, a magic thread,
We weave the comfortable with fun instead.

In ordinary chaos, joys arise,
Wrapped in laughter, a sweet surprise.
For in the echoes, we find the grace,
Of wonders hidden in each place.

Between the Lines of the Complex

In tangled knots of thoughts we see,
The laughter lurking, wild and free.
For every puzzle we try to solve,
More questions dance, they just revolve.

A riddle wrapped in quirky lines,
Like dot-to-dots that twist and twine.
"Why is this blue?" "Why's that a cat?"
The answers play, like chips in a spat.

So here we stand, amidst the snare,
With lines that cross, they seem unfair.
Yet with a wink and silly grin,
We learn to laugh where doubts begin.

Let's flip the script, break the mold,
In comedy's grip, we will not fold.
For in the maelstrom, we'll find our cheer,
In every twist, we'll persevere.

Finding Order in the Wild

In the forest of socks, I roam,
Chasing lost mates, far from home.
Found a shoe, but where's the pair?
A quest for order, I shall dare.

Nature whispers, 'Just embrace the mess,'
But my closet screams, 'Can we do less?'
A lion's roar or a cat's soft purr,
Which one fits this wardrobe blur?

I bumped into my dust bunny crew,
They say, 'We're comfy—join us too!'
With tangled vines of thoughts, I laugh,
Is this the path? Or just a gaffe?

Yet amid the chaos, there's delight,
Sipping tea while I sort the fight.
Each odd sock holds a story dear,
In this wild, I find my cheer!

The Knot of Everyday Choices

Coffee or tea? That's a daily grind,
A choice that leaves me half-defined.
To sew or to knit? Wait, what's the plan?
Knots in my mind—a creative jam.

Daily dilemmas wrap me tight,
Boring cereal or an omelette bright?
Tangled in options, I scratch my head,
"Is toast too much? I'll skip the bread."

With each tiny choice, my brain does twist,
A sip of confusion in morning mist.
Should I jog, or just nap instead?
Decisions weighing much like lead.

Yet in this knot, there's joy to find,
Unexpected fun sparks in my mind.
The dance of choices makes me grin,
Maybe simplicity is the real win!

Clockwork Hearts and Twisted Paths

Ticking clocks and hearts that race,
Chasing dreams at a frantic pace.
Do I follow my heart's loud laugh,
Or stick to paths carved on my behalf?

The clock says 'run' but my feet say 'stay',
Do I wear blue, or is red okay?
With every twist, the plot unwinds,
In the maze of thought, confusion binds.

Should I dance like no one sees?
Or keep it cool with minimal ease?
Clockwork friends with strange, chirpy voices,
Tell me my heart's made up of choices.

Embracing the chaos like a pro,
Who knew confusion could steal the show?
With each funny turn, I learn to start,
The beauty lies in a twisted heart!

Mosaic of Moments

Moments scattered like confetti bright,
Stuck in my hair, yet a joyful sight.
A clumsy dance in the grocery aisle,
Is that my cart or do I just smile?

Every laugh a piece of the scene,
A puzzle made from the everyday routine.
Tripping on dreams, I often say,
'This whirlwind joy is the best buffet!'

With quirky friends and a coffee spree,
Each sip a splash of absurdity.
Mismatched socks and a well-timed joke,
Create a patchwork—what fun we soak!

So here's to the quirks that paint our days,
Life spins a tale in the funniest ways.
Embrace the chaos and let it flow,
In this wacky mosaic, together we glow!

Laughing at the Labyrinth

In a maze of choices, I walk with glee,
Every turn is an option, oh joy, c'est la vie!
Yet I trip on my thoughts, like a clown at a fair,
Wondering if life's just a cosmic affair.

With signs that point every which way but right,
I smile at my fate, and dance through the night.
Do I go left for dinner or right for dessert?
Maybe it's just cake that I need to convert!

Round and round like a hamster on wheels,
The answer eludes me, but oh, how it feels!
I'm a jester of choices with punchlines galore,
Chuckling at chaos while searching for more.

So here in the labyrinth, I prance with delight,
Collecting my laughter through all of the fright.
With jumbled decisions like confetti they fall,
Who says this perplexity isn't a ball?

Echoes of the Unfathomable

I ponder the universe, a riddle supreme,
Where fish might fly and cows plot a scheme.
Questions aplenty, like socks without pairs,
In this baffling dance, we tumble down stairs.

With echoes that whisper, then playfully shout,
Is number twelve really what it's all about?
I find my lost marbles, they roll out of sight,
But oh, how they twinkle, they're quite the delight!

In this jumble of wonders, I trip and I fall,
Chasing my thoughts like a ball in a brawl.
With quirky conclusions and laughter to boot,
I leap through the chaos in a giant pink suit!

So here we all giggle at mysteries grand,
As we juggle the serious and throw out a hand.
With echoes of nonsense, we dance in a line,
For the baffling twists are truly divine!

The Dance of the Unseen

In shadows we twirl, where no one can see,
The groovy step secrets that set our minds free.
Each twist brings a giggle, each twirl adds delight,
As we moonwalk through problems that vanish from sight.

The partners are unknown, the rhythm's a blast,
We shuffle through chaos, forgetting the past.
With invisible dance floors and laughs flowing bright,
Who needs a plan when you can jump at the light?

We twinkle like stars that just popped up for fun,
With the universe spinning, we've barely begun.
So waltz with your worries, let's cha-cha your scheme,
In the dance of the unseen, we laugh and we beam!

As the music plays on, what a sight to behold,
We flip misunderstanding to laughter and gold.
So let's jive through the night without a trace,
In this wacky performance, we all find our place!

Uncharted Waters

I sail on a sea where directions are rare,
With waves of confusion and fish in my hair.
Each splash is a question, each gust a surprise,
As I steer through the whims of the great, big blue skies.

The compass spins wildly like a top in a dream,
Do I follow the clouds or the glittering beam?
With sharks in tuxedos and octopuses' flair,
It's a party at sea, I can't help but stare.

I toss out my map, embrace the unknown,
With laughter the anchor, I happily roam.
In these uncharted waters, the joys are a feast,
Each wave brings a giggle, a tale at least!

So let the wind guide me, wherever it blows,
With whimsy as my captain, let's see how it goes.
No need for a chart in this flutter of fun,
For the journey itself is the absolute run!

Layers of the Every Day

Peeling back my morning toast,
I find a layer of burnt ghost.
Forgot the eggs, they're half a rock,
But what the heck, I'll have a sock!

Socks on feet, but not a pair,
Chasing cats; they simply stare.
Coffee spills, my hair's a mess,
Yet I still smile, I guess that's best.

Emails pile, a mountain high,
Searching for a simple hi.
Sale alerts are like a tease,
Who knew that shopping could be a breeze?

At the end, I take a bow,
Life's a circus, anyhow.
With laughter echoing all around,
In this chaos, joy is found.

Beyond the Veil of Confusion

Woke up late, forgot my pants,
Tripping over careless prance.
Mystery of lost car keys,
Turns out they're in cheese unease!

Maps we follow, lost at sea,
Directions marked with "maybe."
Taking turns on little whims,
Navigating life on a whimsy whim.

Staplers jam, and printers sigh,
I wave hello, the postman's shy.
Juggling tasks like mangled fruit,
Yet here I stand, with time to boot.

Every day a curious jest,
Underneath it, feel the zest.
In the chaos, I find my place,
Among the silly, I keep pace.

The Jigsaw of Our Journeys

Pieces scattered, what's the fit?
Trying hard, I lose a bit.
Who knew puzzles had such glee?
Twists and turns of you and me.

At brunch tables, crumbs abound,
While laughter's echoing all around.
Take a sip and drop the cake,
It's just a smile, for goodness' sake!

Paths we tread, with shoes mismatched,
Accidentally style attached.
Life's a riddle, troubadour,
Dancing like it's meant for four.

Final piece, I hold it near,
With a grin, I face the cheer.
Jigsaw dreams a bit askew,
But mixed-up joy sees me through.

Shadows in the Light of Clarity

Caught in sunlight, oh so bright,
Shadows dance in silly flight.
Thinking deep, but what's the score?
Is it a riddle or a chore?

I wear my pants inside out,
Strutting proudly, twirl about.
Like a wizard lost in spells,
Confusion fits, oh, how it dwells!

Voices echo, "What's the plan?"
I shrug and laugh, a simple man.
The truth is silly if you peek,
In every laugh, o' joy we seek.

So here's a toast, to all the fun,
To shadows danced and chaos spun.
In this bright yet hazy air,
We find our joy, without a care.

Fragile Moments of Clarity

A bird sings sweetly, yet trips on a wire,
Chasing the wind, as if it's on fire.
We juggle our thoughts, they tumble and fall,
Like ice cream cones melting, we savor it all.

In a crowded café, your order is wrong,
You laugh it off, joining the throng.
Each mix-up's a hint, a joyful delight,
As we sip on our drinks, hearts ready to flight.

A sock on a floor, keeps you awake,
You ponder its story, the choices they make.
Fragile moments whisper, between laughter and tears,
Solve one riddle, lose track of the years.

With wisdom like jelly, it wobbles and spins,
Crafting our puzzles, we giggle at sins.
In chaos and order, we dance like a flame,
Fragile moments of clarity, never the same.

Simplistic Illusions

A butterfly lands on a step of the stair,
We ponder its journey, but don't really care.
It flutters and teases, just out of our reach,
While we sip from our coffee, a mysterious peach.

A cat in a box, seems wise beyond days,
While humans just lose track in their maze.
We question existence with each silly shrug,
As reality giggles and gives us a hug.

A fortune cookie whispers, 'Your luck is divine,'
As you fumble your keys, for the third time at nine.
We chuckle at life, in this hilarious spree,
With simplistic illusions we're just a movie.

Wrapped in our thoughts, they swim like a fish,
It's funny how simple, becomes quite a wish.
In laughter and chaos, we twirl in delight,
Our minds like confetti, in whimsical flight.

Shades of a Simple Smile

A toddler's giggle, so pure, so bright,
Spills over chaos, painting the night.
In mismatched old socks, we find common ground,
A simple smile dances, where joy can be found.

The dog with a shoe, a riddle untold,
Mimics our journeys, the brave and the bold.
We laugh as he struts, like royalty proud,
In shades of delight, we join in the crowd.

The coffee is cold, the toast is all burnt,
Yet we share a chuckle, no lessons to learn.
Together we weave through the quirks and the fun,
In the tapestry woven, there dwell our son.

With smiles like umbrellas, we weather the storm,
Finding joy in the simple, embracing the warm.
Through twists and turns, we'll glide, never stop,
In shades of a simple smile, laughter on top.

The Art of Overthinking

In a room filled with thoughts, our minds twist and twine,

We ponder and ponder, could it be just fine?
Over coffee and crumbs, we unravel the spree,
In a quest for solutions, we flee from the free.

A dinner invite throws us into a spin,
What to wear, what to eat, where to begin?
We craft every word, in elaborate verse,
As our minds start to waddle, we pray not to burst.

The clock ticks in laughter, as seconds float by,
We fret over choices, like raisins in pie.
In the chart of our heads, we scribble and doodle,
While humor pokes fun at our own mental noodle.

With worries like bubbles, they rise and they pop,
In the art of overthinking, we twist and we flop.
Yet amidst all the chaos, we smile 'til it's late,
For laughter's the answer to the threads that we rate.

The Curves of Life's Highway

With speed bumps that jolt and sway,
We navigate in a quirky way.
Sometimes lost, but that's just fine,
We laugh it off with a glass of wine.

Roundabouts that spin around,
Making sense can feel unfound.
Yet in the chaos, smiles appear,
As giggles echo loud and clear.

Exit signs that tease and taunt,
Should we stop or just fawn?
We buckle up, hold on tight,
For joy is found in the silly plight.

So take a turn and don't look back,
In this crazy funny track.
Embrace the ride, let out a cheer,
For twists and turns bring laughter near.

Riddles Wrapped in Routine

Every morning starts the same,
With coffee brewed, oh what a game!
Socks mismatched on purposeful feet,
A puzzle piece that feels quite neat.

Emails ping with tales absurd,
Routine seems like a slumbering bird.
Yet in the mundane, surprises lurk,
Like finding a treasure in your work.

Lunch breaks filled with quirky quirks,
Office banter and playful smirks.
We juggle tasks, some might collide,
In the rhythm, fun must abide.

At five o'clock, we clock out fast,
Leaving seriousness in the past.
Riddles of routine, we solve with flair,
In this carousel of laughter, we share.

The Beauty in the Baffled

Oh, look at the puzzle pieces stray,
Confusion dances in a funny way.
With mismatched thoughts and scattered glee,
The beauty lives in what we can't see.

Scrambled eggs and thoughts askew,
Who knew the morning would feel so blue?
Yet laughter comes when we embrace,
The silly turns we often face.

Friends gather 'round to share a laugh,
In baffled moments, we find our path.
With stories that twist in the telling,
The joy of the jumbled is quite compelling.

So here's to the beauty, oh so grand,
In the baffled moments, we boldly stand.
For in the chaos, bonds ignite,
And laughter shines, a guiding light.

Fragments of Fathomable

Thoughts like bubbles, floating high,
Drifting by in a colorful sky.
Each pop reveals a curious truth,
In fragments found, we reclaim our youth.

Nonsense riddles, what do they mean?
Life's questions dance, a playful scene.
With jumbled bits and laughter raw,
In puzzling pieces, there's fun galore.

Connecting dots in abstract ways,
Like scribbles turning into a maze.
In this canvas, humor's the key,
Unlocking joy in hilarity.

So let's embrace the puzzle's art,
In every piece, there lies a heart.
For in the fragmented, we find our song,
A joyful melody, where we belong.

Existential Jigsaw

Pieces scattered everywhere,
Trying to fit them right,
Why's this edge a corner?
Is that star a bolt of light?

Puzzle's missing half its face,
Turns out, it's just the cat,
He's lounging in the box,
What a complicated brat!

I twist and turn, oh what a flair,
Boxes piling up in stacks,
A marvel's hidden deep in there,
Or maybe just some snacks?

So I sit and scratch my head,
Why does this need to rhyme?
The jigsaw waits for me, instead,
I've lost track of my time!

The Simplicity Paradox

Here's a sandwich, plain as day,
But what's this spread inside?
A dash of joy, a pinch of play,
And yet, it all collides!

A sunny side-up egg on toast,
Is breakfast really grand?
Or just a simple chore, at most,
In a chaotic land?

The mug's just full of steaming brew,
But look—there's whipped cream!
What's simple seems so hard to do,
Am I lost in this dream?

Chasing answers down the street,
While birds fly overhead,
Oh, funny how our lives repeat,
Is this all in my head?

Tangles of the Everyday

My shoelaces tell me tales,
Of running late for trains,
They twist and tie, take windy trails,
Then laugh at all my pains.

Laundry's a never-ending game,
Where socks play hide and seek,
Each cycle's just a wild flame,
Of wrinkled clothes so bleak!

Coffee spills, a morning jest,
A dance beneath the sun,
I scrub the floor, a quirky quest,
But is this really fun?

As I untangle all these threads,
I giggle at the plot,
For chaos spins within my head,
It's all quite a hotshot!

Whispers in a Chaotic World

The traffic hums an anxious tune,
As I sip my mango shake,
With phone in hand, I'm lost in gloom,
And drop the cake I bake.

In queues we stand, all glued in place,
What dish do I want now?
I'm ready to toss the agitated pace,
But wait—it's taco chow!

Puppies bark while kids run wild,
With ice cream dripping down,
Yet in this mess, there lies a smile,
As chaos swoops and drowns.

Beneath the whispers, 'what to do?'
I learn to laugh at fate,
For in this world of crazy blue,
I'm dancing through the gates!

A Symphony of Small Moments

A squirrel steals my sandwich, oh what a sight,
Running with haste, in pure delight.
The sun makes a shadow, a dance on the dirt,
While I ponder if mustard was the right choice of shirt.

The cat knocks a vase, it shatters with flair,
While I sip my coffee, pretend not to care.
A bird sings a tune that I can't quite recall,
Maybe it's saying, 'Just have a ball.'

A child asks deep questions, like why is the sky?
I'm stumped and just shrug, with a twinkling eye.
Yet in these small moments, simple and bright,
Complexities vanish, laughter takes flight.

With giggles and mishaps, we sway to the beat,
Collecting these instances, oh what a treat.
So here's to the chaos, the silly and fun,
A symphony crafted, way before we've begun.

Sketches of Serendipity

I tripped on a curb, met the mailman mid-air,
We shared an odd laugh, it lightened my care.
A dog stole my shoe as I chased after it,
Life's quirks make a canvas of pure misfit.

A sandwich lands face-down, with a cartoonish splat,
I sigh and I chuckle, how silly is that?
Two birds made a fuss, a brawl at the tree,
Who knew that such drama could happen for free?

Caught in a tumble, I befriended a snail,
Who whispered sweet secrets about life's funny trail.
Each twist of the day, a masterpiece bold,
Sketching our stories, both vibrant and gold.

So let's toast to the stumble, the awkward and surreal,
Raise a glass to the moments that oddly appeal.
For in these quick sketches, joy finds its way,
A tale of serendipity, brightening our day.

The Paradox We Inhabit

I lose my keys while I'm holding them tight,
They laugh from my pocket, what a silly fright!
The calendar mocks me, it says I'm late,
While I stand by the door, checking the date.

A puzzle with pieces that never align,
As I brew my coffee, it bubbles with wine.
I search for my pen, it's tucked in my ear,
It's quite a conundrum, this thing we call here.

The clock ticks away while I dance in a chair,
My cat gives a shrug, with a look full of flair.
We wrestle with answers that never appear,
Yet we laugh at the riddle, it's all part of the cheer.

In this topsy-turvy, humorous sprawl,
We ponder the silly, the big and the small.
So come join the chaos, embrace the delight,
For the paradox holds us, both merry and bright.

Reflections in the Mind's Mirror

I glance in the mirror, and what do I see?
A hair that's rebellious, just like it's free.
The toothpaste is splattered, a canvas of white,
Good thing I'm not worried; I'm in for a fight.

A jog through the park, where I trip on a stone,
And twist my own thoughts, feeling quite alone.
But laughter erupts with a squirrel's acrobat,
Who knows that in life, we're all a bit flat.

A book lies open, the cover is torn,
Words tumble like daisies, all rumpled and worn.
Yet in each little miss, a lesson is sown,
Reflections remind me, I'm never alone.

So dance with the quirks and embrace all the fun,
Although we may falter, we shine like the sun.
With joy in the chaos, our laughter runs clear,
In reflections we find what we hold most dear.

Mist on a Summer's Morning

In the dawn, the mist confounds,
A squirrel checkers, zigzags 'round.
Coffee spills, a cat leaps high,
Birds debate the cloud-strewn sky.

A toast to toast, it's burnt again,
Chasing sunshine, dodging rain.
Did I leave the fridge agape?
Such is the gamble of escape!

Butterflies dance, a breeze in tow,
Forget the map, just let it go.
Sunrise paints a silly grin,
What's lost can always blur back in!

Life's a puzzle with missing bits,
Yet laughter's spark ignites our wits.
A riddle spun in morning's light,
All's well, let's frolic in delight.

Destined to Overcomplicate

With each new plan, the web expands,
Doodles, diagrams, and rubber bands.
Why take a stroll when we can run?
I lost the race, but oh, what fun!

Cereal's too crunchy, tea's too hot,
Why did I think I'd grow a plot?
Maps are fickle, my phone's outsmarted,
The quest for simple, I've dearly charted.

Got a box of jumbled thoughts,
Tangled wires and tangled knots.
Every answer leads to more,
Why do I open that closed door?

In chaos, the humor shows its face,
Every blunder, a comic grace.
Simpler paths, they tease and mock,
But what's the fun without the shock?

Playful Chaos in Stillness

Underneath the calm façade,
Lies a dance of thoughts, quite mad.
Juggling dreams, a tempting feat,
The world is still, but oh, so sweet!

Kids chase bubbles, they laugh and fall,
While ants march off to their own ball.
I ponder deeply while I bake,
Should it be pie or chocolate cake?

Inside my head, a circus plays,
Fire-breathers of sunny rays.
Chasing order? Now that's a joke,
My pillow's got the wisest cloak!

In playful chaos, wisdom swirls,
Laughter lifts, and joy unfurls.
Why strive for calm when chaos sings?
It's here that my heart leaps and springs!

Mirth of Simple Joys

A bubble gum balloon takes flight,
As laughter shatters the silent night.
Caught in a game of tag with peers,
The best of times, not best of fears.

Raindrops play a symphony sweet,
Kicking puddles with bare feet.
Silly hats and mismatched socks,
Finding treasure in mundane blocks.

A wink from fate, a twist of chance,
Stumbling in a happy dance.
Why not sing off-key today?
Life's a stage, and we're here to play!

With simple pleasures comes delight,
Chasing sunsets, holding tight.
In laughter's arms we find our way,
To marvel at the bright array.

The Enigma of Ordinary Days

In the morning, toast burns bright,
Coffee spills with sheer delight.
Socks don mismatched dance,
Who knew chaos had a chance?

Plans are written on a whim,
Yet nothing seems to fit the brim.
The cat knocks over the plant,
Oh, what a charming little rant!

A soup spills like a grand parade,
Yet laughter keeps the mess at bay.
Each moment's like a riddle spun,
Isn't this just so much fun?

As we trip on tiny whims,
Every stumble, every grin.
Pretty patterns made of strife,
Oh, what a curious life!

Twists and Turns of Trust

A friend insists they'll take the lead,
Yet shows up only to misread.
Plans are tangled like old yarn,
Trust is sweet, but oft a charm.

We sign up for a noon-time jog,
But end up lost, or in a fog.
Expectations take a twisty turn,
Lessons learned, and still we yearn.

With every promise ever made,
Comes a little price thus paid.
Yet we laugh through every mess,
In trust's embrace, we never stress.

So in life's game of hide and seek,
Find the joy in every freak.
Trust is tricky, yet so fun,
Together we will always run!

A Light Breeze on Heavy Thoughts

Heavy thoughts can weigh me down,
Yet giggles keep me off the ground.
A breeze comes dancing through my hair,
Oh look, a butterfly! How rare!

We ponder deep while sipping tea,
Contemplating what it's meant to be.
Philosophy or silly games,
Who knew we'd dance with silly names?

In every thought, a feather glides,
As laughter goes on joyous rides.
Light hearts lift those troubled eyes,
As happiness becomes our prize.

So here's to all the crazy schemes,
And laughter echoing like dreams.
Heavy thoughts, take a chill pill,
For laughter is the heart's true thrill!

Frayed Edges of Clarity

I once sought truths in tidy rows,
Yet life unraveled, much to my woes.
The neatest plans just fell apart,
What's simple, dear, inside the heart?

The answers flicker like a flame,
Each insight feels a little lame.
In messy strokes, we find our way,
Clarified through laughter's play.

If clarity comes in tangled strands,
Then humor lights both empty hands.
We laugh at what we cannot see,
A frayed thread, perhaps it's meant to be.

So here's to comfort in the blur,
To finding joy in what we stir.
In chaos, beauty finds its place,
Frayed edges weave a fun embrace!

The Art of Second Guesses

I woke up today with a plan in my head,
Only to trip on my shoelace instead.
The coffee was burning, my toast was a flop,
Yet here I am laughing, juggling the swap.

I thought I'd be wise, wearing wisdom's disguise,
But tripped on my thoughts, oh how time flies!
Decisions like pancakes, flip-flopping around,
Completing my breakfast, confusion profound.

Maps with no routes, and plans that go south,
I giggle and ponder, oh what's it about?
A dance through the chaos, I'll take it all slow,
With chuckles and wiggles, and a bright, sunny glow.

So here's to the mess, and to whimsical turns,
For every odd question, a new lesson burns.
Embrace all the quirky, the weird, and the wild,
In this art of second guesses, we're all but a child.

Breezes of Bewilderment

A butterfly landed, then flew off too quick,
I waved to my neighbor, he blinked—I felt sick.
The sun said hello, then hid behind clouds,
Weather forecasters lost in their crowds.

At breakfast this morning, my cereal swam,
Singing a tune like it's part of a jam.
An orange said 'hello,' while the apple just smiled,
In hindsight, it seemed more than a bit wild.

I walked down the street, puzzled and blind,
A cat chased its tail, oh what did it find?
The wind whispered secrets, while I tried to speak,
To the mailbox that giggled—my week was quite bleak.

So here's to the breezes, and flutters of fun,
To the twirls in our steps and the shines of the sun.
For who really knows what's up or what's down,
When we're dancing through bewilderment, grinning, not frown.

The Narrative of Unfolding Beauty

Puzzles scattered on the floor, all askew,
Trying to fit pieces, but which goes with who?
A portrait of laughter overflowing my cup,
Oh wait, there's the cat—she's flipping it up!

The flowers are blooming, but some are in gray,
While ants march in line, just leading the way.
Sunshine and shadows, a dance on the wall,
Where's my lost sock? Oh—there goes my call!

Every colorful moment, a tale to be told,
With giggles and wiggles, and laughter of old.
The world spins around, a carousel bright,
In this vibrant narrative, all's strangely right.

So let's throw confetti, and celebrate cheer,
Embrace the absurd and release every fear.
For beauty lies hidden in moments askew,
In the narrative of life, it's wonderfully true.

Reflections of the Heart's Labyrinth

A mirror gave me winks, oh what a tease,
I laughed at my hair, doing just as it pleased.
Two steps to the left, just to lose my way,
In this heart's maze, every corner's at play.

Thoughts bouncing like bunnies, now where do they go?
One said it's easy, another said no.
Through twists of confusion, I find little clues,
As echoes of giggles bring colorful hues.

The walls of my worries are painted in cheer,
With tapestries woven from laughter and fear.
It's a dance in a maze, a jig of the soul,
With each quirky pitfall, I'm taking a toll.

So here's to reflections, and moments that twist,
Where joy's in the journey, not where you missed.
For in this heart's labyrinth, so wild and so bright,
I'll find all the wonders, wrapped up in delight.

Dancing in the Gray

In the murky middle, we twirl and spin,
Where laughter tickles and chases the din.
We wear mismatched socks, a hat on our head,
And step on the dog as we dance without dread.

With each silly shimmy, we shrug off the frown,
As clouds play peek-a-boo, pretending to drown.
We sip on confusion, a cocktail of cheer,
And find that our worries have vanished from here.

A waltz with the chaos, a jig through the mud,
Our folly's a rhythm, a hop and a thud.
In a world painted gray, we splatter with glee,
Finding merriment where others don't see.

So let the drums roll and the trumpets all blast,
We'll dance in this haze, forget about fast.
For in silly steps, we uncover the fun,
While spinning in gray, we know we've all won.

Threads of Confusion

Tangled up blankets on cold winter nights,
We weave our own stories, with humorous sights.
With knitting gone haywire, oh what a delight,
The sweater for Grandma looks more like a kite.

With a stitch here and there, we puzzle it through,
Craft a life so silly, who knew it so flew?
We laugh at our failures, make yarn bombs of pride,
While socks shrink to mittens in this goofy ride.

Confusion's a friend that we welcome with glee,
Wrapped up in our threads, it's a grand jubilee.
A tapestry woven with giggles and fear,
We stitch up the chaos and it all becomes clear.

In this world of knotted strings, we take up the thread,
Spin yarns of the baffled, our hearts widely spread.
With needles of laughter, we create our own fate,
Through threads of confusion, we celebrate great.

Pleasantries in Complexity

In the maze of our minds, we dance in delight,
Securing our sanity with every odd bite.
The recipe calls for a dash of perplex,
A sprinkle of fun, or just stick to the hex.

We juggle with creatures of thought on parade,
Mix improbable flavors, the outcome's a trade.
With a splash of mistakes, a dollop of cheer,
We feast on the puzzling, the taste buds sincere.

Like origami swans that fold into laughs,
Our simplicity hides in the complex staffs.
A yawn turns to giggles, confusion a friend,
We savor the oddness, come join 'til the end.

So let's toast to the tricky, the wild joy we share,
In this banquet of riddles, there's plenty to spare.
Amidst all the puzzles, we see the bright side,
In pleasures of chaos, we dance like the tide.

The Puzzle of Each Breath

Inhale with a giggle, exhale with a grin,
Every breath's a puzzle, where chaos begins.
We play with our lungs as we breathe in delight,
A riddle of air that takes flight in the night.

With hiccups and chuckles, we stumble and sway,
A symphony wobbles as thoughts drift astray.
Count breaths like sheep, then realize the fact,
Each one's a question we merrily hack.

The rhythm of life is a curious jest,
We chase after answers, but find we're not pressed.
In the game of existence, it's silly and clear,
With each breath we take, the fun's in the fear.

So let every gasp be a giggle's delight,
Play hopscotch with air through the day and the night.
For in puzzles of breath, we sincerely connect,
Finding joy in the chaos, our hearts will reflect.

Navigating the Maze of Being

There's a map in my head, yet I seem to stray,
Chasing my tail in a humorous way.
Dodging the corners, I take a wrong turn,
Laughing at lessons that I still have to learn.

Friends suggest shortcuts; they always misspeak,
When I try to follow, I just feel so meek.
Life is a puzzle, with pieces that shift,
I'd rather be playing; it's all about gifts.

Round and round on this merry-go-round,
Whirling in circles, I never feel bound.
Taking a step, I still trip on my laces,
But oh, what a joy when I see smiling faces.

So here's to the chaos and silly mistakes,
Embracing the quirks that the journey makes.
In the maze of my being, I laugh and I cheer,
For with every misstep, I gather good cheer.

The Illusion of Simplicity

Oh sure, they say 'simple,' I nod and I grin,
But unraveling knots feels like drawing within.
Like a sandwich with layers I can't quite discern,
Each bite brings a twist, for lessons I yearn.

A straight line, they claim, from point A to B,
Yet I zigzag and wiggle like a fish in the sea.
I strategize hard, always plotting and scheming,
Only to stumble on my own convoluting dreaming.

With rules laid out, I turn them around,
In logic's tight grip, I've fearfully drowned.
Yet humor arises from the mess that I make,
A quirk in the plan leads to laughs for my sake.

Perhaps it's the riddle of this funny charade,
A topsy-turvy world where clear paths seem to fade.
So I'll dance through the chaos, with grace and with glee,
For the sweet taste of laughter is the key, don't you see?

When Serenity Meets Chaos

In the quiet of morning, I sip on my tea,
But the universe chuckles, 'You'll wait just to see!'
A squirrel steals my muffin, a bird claims my chair,
Serene moments vanish, like they weren't even there.

With a deep breath I gather my zen-like resolve,
Yet socks on the floor seem far from absolved.
Oh, the bliss of a moment turns comedic instead,
When chaos insists I'm just losing my head!

With the rhythm of laughter, I skip through the fray,
Serenity whispers, 'Just make each joke play.'
Whether juggling schedules or newly found grime,
I'll dance with the madness and find peace each time.

So bring on the chaos, I'll giggle and sway,
For with each twist and turn comes a bright brand-new day.
In the realm of the nutty, I thrive and I beam,
As the waves of absurdity tighten my dream.

A Dance of Contradictions

I'm happy yet grumpy, I'm lost but I'm found,
On this dance floor of life where the contradictions abound.
One minute I'm soaring, then tripping on air,
With a grin on my face, it's all part of the flair.

I chase after fortune, then trip on a dime,
Wrestling with fortune like it's some sort of crime.
Is it foolishness rising or wisdom deployed?
Laughing in circles, I feel so overjoyed.

Balancing plans with spontaneous bliss,
In this funky tango, I can't help but miss.
Eluding my straight path, I wobble and sway,
With contradictions embraced, I dance through the fray.

As I whirl with confusion, I find my beat sweet,
With the harmony of oddities moving my feet.
In the dance of existence, I twirl and I spin,
For each step in this ballet invites joy to begin.

Navigating the Cosmic Dance

Stars wink at my steps,
As I trip on moonbeams.
Navigating this cosmic dance,
With mismatched socks, it seems.

Gravity pulls at my jokes,
They fall flat like pancakes.
I stumble through stellar themes,
Laughter's all that it makes.

In orbit around my dreams,
Rockets powered by giggles.
Asteroids made of old schemes,
They crash with cosmic wiggles.

Yet here I float in the void,
With a grin that's out of place.
Each twirl a joy, not destroyed,
Just a laugh in space's embrace.

The Weight of the Light

Sunbeams spill on my face,
Like butter on toast, oh so smooth.
Chasing shadows, what a race,
As giggles start to soothe.

Clouds carry my worries high,
Like balloons in a child's hand.
They pop when I laugh and cry,
And drift in a whimsical land.

The sun wears funky sunglasses,
A star with style and flair.
It dances in fun little classes,
Training clouds to be rare.

Amidst the weight of the light,
I skip through each funny phase.
Finding humor in the fight,
With sunshine that brightly plays.

The Unraveling Cloth of Days

Threads of time tangle tight,
As I knit my daily fun.
Each stitch a giggle in sight,
Underneath the warming sun.

Parades of socks misaligned,
Dance in the fabric of hours.
Laughter's what we really find,
In this stranding of powers.

The spool keeps rolling away,
Chasing the yarn with delight.
We weave the chaos each day,
And spin it into the light.

So let the seams come undone,
We'll patch them with joy and cheer.
In this fabric, we've all won,
As unraveling brings us near.

Chasing Shadows of Certainty

I run after shadows long,
With a flashlight that's out of juice.
The dance turns into a song,
As I laugh and cut loose.

With questions that swirl around,
Like confetti in the wind.
Each answer feels like a clown,
That slips through, unpinned.

I leap over doubts and fears,
Tripping on truths that are spry.
These moments dissolve in cheers,
While the stars wink from the sky.

In this chase, I light the way,
With a grin that never dims.
The shadows play hide and seek,
But laughter always wins.

Eclipsed by the Apparent

I tie my shoes but trip instead,
Why is the world a constant thread?
The sun shines bright, yet clouds will play,
Navigating silliness every day.

I seek the path, then lose my way,
A squirrel's dance, it steals the day.
I ponder deep over simple tasks,
Is it clarity or just a mask?

I wave at cars, they don't respond,
The cat looks regal, an endless bond.
Oh, wisdom claims few secrets spill,
Yet I misplace my car keys at will!

In jokes we find a hint, a clue,
What's normal here and what is new?
When laughter strikes, the answers hide,
Is it folly, or a clever guide?

Illuminating the Confusion

I juggle thoughts like pebbles tossed,
In laughter's glow, my sanity's lost.
A compass spins, it knows no aim,
In my brain's hall of endless shame.

Oh, tick tock goes the clock so loud,
My plans dissolve, they're not allowed.
With every step, I find my fall,
The punchline's waiting; I must recall.

We search for truths beneath the mist,
As fortune cookies clench a fist.
I'll dance with doubts, embrace the strange,
For who knows what's within that change?

In moonlit whimsy, we laugh away,
The chaos turns to a light ballet.
Here's to confusion's lovely art,
A riddle wrapped in giggles, bright and tart!

The Puzzle of Existence

A puzzle box with missing pieces,
I ask my friends, yet confusion increases.
Why is popcorn an art form here?
With butter dreams and sticky cheer.

Do fish consider the air too dense?
As I ponder thoughts so immense.
With every question, giggles bloom,
An irony drifts through every room.

I lost my phone in the fridge it seems,
Reality plays with the silliest themes.
With laughter thick as honey spreads,
I click my pen, and it gently treads.

As colors swirl in nonsensical ways,
The world turns bright through cowardly days.
In jokes, I find the missing clues,
Is it wisdom, or just playful blues?

Simple Threads

From tangled yarn, my sweater grows,
But where it ends, nobody knows.
I knit my dreams while sipping tea,
A pattern lost, what could it be?

With mismatched socks and laughter loud,
I dance through life, not too proud.
Perplexity flirts, it makes me tease,
And tickles thoughts like gentle breeze.

The sun will rise as shadows chase,
In silly games, we find our place.
Do we chase answers or just giggles?
A quirky smile as the world wiggles.

So let's unwind this rope of fate,
A tapestry where threads are straight.
In joy, we find the purest blend,
That simple things will always mend.

Tangled Patterns

I'm caught in webs of thought unclear,
A jester's court, with laughter near.
Do socks have souls? I often muse,
While tangled tales amuse the blues.

In paradoxes, my heart can leap,
As questions swirl, the answers creep.
Oh, how the spins of fortune play,
Like juggling dreams at the close of day.

In mismatched dance, the chaos sways,
Our fumbles echo, a sweet ballet.
With every twist, a giggle breaks,
In simplicity, a laughter wakes.

So let the patterns laugh and wail,
For life's a ride, a curious trail.
We'll laugh together through this show,
With tangled threads, we learn and grow.

www.ingramcontent.com/pod-product-compliance
Lightning Source LLC
Chambersburg PA
CBHW051650160426
43209CB00004B/854